FROM SOLDIER TO DOCTOR

DR RATILAL GOVINDBHAI

FROM

SOLDIER

TO

DOCTOR

A JOURNEY THROUGH LIFE OF HARDSHIP & HARD WORK

Published by Mzayifani Clive Sibanda using Reach Publishers' services,
P O Box 1384, Wandsbeck, South Africa, 3631

Edited by Gerard Peter for Reach Publishers
Cover designed by Reach Publishers
Website: www.reachpublishers.org
E-mail: reach@reachpublishers.org

DR MZAYIFANI CLIVE SIBANDA

clivem.cs@gmail.com

This small memoir is dedicated to all those who have supported me throughout the years of my life's struggles. I would like to thank my parents, Mr PJ Sibanda (God Rest His Soul) and Mrs CM Sibanda, who ensured that even through the hardships, learning had to take place. They made sure that I went to school regardless of the poverty situation at home. To my family – my late wife (God Rest Her Soul) and my beautiful daughters, I want to say thank you for understanding that Daddy needed to do this, which meant that there was less time to spend with you, especially at the beginning of the Master's and PhD journeys. You have been a great support and I appreciate it.

This book is meant to encourage those who are on the verge of giving up on their careers due to challenges and stumbling blocks in life. I want to say to them that a journey to success is never easy, you need to keep pushing and endure. I managed to get to where I am using the 3D Principle (dedication, determination and discipline). It got me this far and I am proud of myself. I hope the little that I am sharing will also do the same for you. Hard work pays off and nothing that is genuine comes easy. You have to struggle and fight to get what is rightfully yours.

Table of Contents

Beginning of the Journey

My journey through life started on 3 July 1972 when I was brought into this world. I was the second of four children and the eldest of the boys. Our parents did not have the opportunity to complete their schooling like they had envisioned. My father had to quit school at JC level (at that time it was Standard 8). Back in the day when you managed to get to JC, you were regarded as clever so my father was among the few that I know who has achieved that. Our parents could not afford to buy a fancy house nor could they afford fancy stuff. They were only qualified to have a normal job like many other parents during the apartheid years. They didn't earn much but it was enough for them to take care of our family. My Father worked as a casual at the SABC and my mother worked in the clothing factory before she joined the belt factory. My father later joined the SANDF and worked as a general worker until he decided to take early retirement at the age of 55 due to ill health.

We lived in a three-room house that was built by the apartheid government. We had a kitchen, one bedroom and a lounge cum bedroom at night. Our parents bought one of those old sleeper couches that me and brother shared at night. My two sisters slept on the bed that was left by my grandmother who passed on in the 1980s. Regardless of the hardships, life carried on as normal. There were days when we went to bed without food and only drank water to keep us going through the night. I remember at times my mother would cook pap and we would add sugar water and down the pap just so we could fill our tummies. The nice thing about this is that no one outside of our home would know that we went to bed hungry at times or know what we had for supper. It was tough but we made it somehow. Mothers will always be mothers and my mother made sure that we didn't starve for the longest time. Even though it was tough, she made it happen somehow.

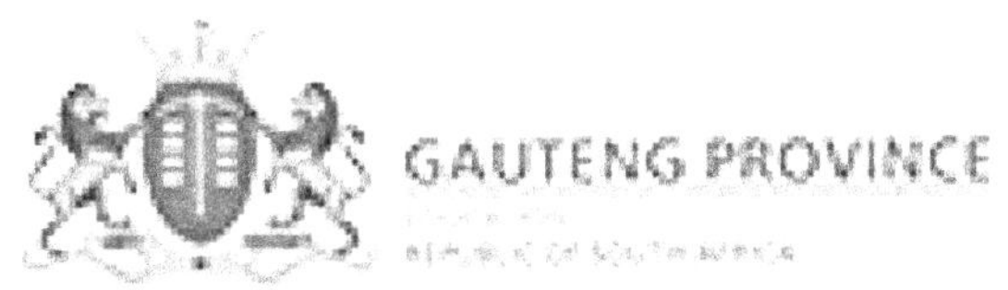

I started my schooling career at the age of seven. In those days, Black children were prohibited from starting school earlier. It didn't matter whether you were smart or not, the age was set by the apartheid government. My late sister, June (God Rest Her Soul), was a year older than me and we used to walk together to school. We attended the same school named Moruta Thuto Lower Primary School. The principal was Mrs Grootboom, a very nice lady who was married to a Coloured and spoke Afrikaans fluently. Ma'am Grootboom, as she was passionately known, took a liking to me and my sister because we also could speak Afrikaans fluently. She was impressed by these young ones who could communicate in Afrikaans so well. My mother is Coloured and somehow this had a bearing on how I would turn out to be when it came to the Afrikaans language. This was advantageous for me and my sister as it made communication in Afrikaans a lot easier. We were the favourites of many teachers because they were fascinated by the fact that we spoke fluent Afrikaans. The principal used to call us to her office during lunch breaks just to have a chat with us. The Afrikaans teacher was also fond of us and protected us most of the time. I guess this was because we could answer her during class and also interacted with her a lot. I do not remember a lot about those years of my life as I was still very young and naive about what was going on in my life. I know for a fact that I was in the school choir as I loved singing from a very early age. We used to go to choir competitions and sing our hearts out. I attended choir practice every Wednesday after school. We used to enjoy the fact that those in the choir were allowed to end classes earlier so that they could go to choir practice. This was an opportunity I could never pass up. It was not like I didn't enjoy school but as a young child, you have those moments where you just want to have every opportunity to be out of the classroom and not sit tediously behind the desk. Growing up during those years taught us valuable lessons in life.

From Moruta Thuto Lower Primary School, I was placed in Tswelelang Higher Primary School. The school was even further than Moruta Thuto and that meant we'd have to wake up very early and travel far to get to school. My late grandmother (God Rest Her Soul), with the help of other learners, negotiated with the principal that we be placed at a school closer to home. This led to our transfer to Tlhokomelo Primary School (now known as Tlhokomelo Special School) which was not such a far walk from home.

TLHOKOMELO
SPECIAL SCHOOL

The principal was Mr Moerane (God rest his soul) and he was very strict. Learners from all over spoke about him because he used to instil discipline in the strictest ways ever. This was the period when corporal punishment was still in full swing. That man was very hard on learners. He loved punishing students during winter time, especially in the mornings while the hands had been exposed to the cold. If you arrived late he would make you stand behind the classrooms and face the sun with your hands stretched out and palms facing up, waiting for your turn to receive your lashes. He used to use a fan belt as a makeshift *sjambok* or a small piece of hosepipe fitted tightly into a piece of steel pipe that he used as a handle. He would normally give you five hard lashes and believe me, after that, you would never come late again. I happened to taste the pain of the hosepipe *sjambok* once only and never did I have to experience it again because I made sure that I never came late again. I think the other times when I experienced corporal punishment was when the school was dirty because the wind blew papers into the yard and the principal found an excuse to punish us for not picking up the papers. The entire school was summoned to the school hall and every single teacher took turns giving us two lashes each. After that day the school was always clean. I was one of the quietest kids in school and always ensured that I stayed out of trouble.

Well, I wasn't all that quiet. I was part of the Afrikaans debating team and we used to beat all the other schools because I could debate with the opposing school with ease. It is a pity I do not have anything to show for it because back in the day, the Bantu education system did not award trophies and other gifts to the winning team. Mr Marera (God rest his soul) was the Afrikaans teacher and he was very fond of me in class as any teacher would be fond of any learner that interacted with them during lessons. He was very good in Afrikaans and he loved his recitation time. He would sit in the back of the class and call a student to go to the front and recite a poem in Afrikaans. He used to make us start from the front left row and progress like that until the whole class had their turn.

If you stood in front of the class and forgot your lines, he would chase you out of the class. His favourite saying was, *"Stap uit, volg"* which simply translated into, "Get out, the next person must follow." We already knew the drill because once he shouted those famous words, you would see a learner run out of the class and the next one jump to the front to start his/her recitation. The reason for chasing us out of the class was for us to go outside and practise the lines again and recite them out loud, over and over again until you felt confident enough and then you could return to class and wait for your turn to be called up again. If you messed up the lines a second time, you would get a hiding because you had an opportunity to go out and practise. I was very fortunate because I knew the poems and I was able to recite them completely. I could then sit down in the class while other learners were outside practising. Mr Marera ended up making me his co-teacher to assist struggling learners to learn their lines. I had moments when I enjoyed this but there were some days I did not because I also wanted to be outside instead of sitting in the class and helping other learners to get a grasp of the recitation. The famous poem that Mr Marera liked was *Muskiete Jag* by A.D. Keet which was as follows:

MUSKIETE JAG by A.D. Keet

Jou vabond, wag, ek sal jou kry,
Van jou sal net 'n bloedkol bly
Hier teen my kamermure.
Deur jou vervloekte gonsery,
Deur jou gebyt en plagery
Kon ek nie slaap vir ure.

Mag ek my voorstel, eer ons skei,
Eer jy die doodslag van my kry –
My naam is van der Merwe.
Muskiet, wees maar nie treurig nie,
Wees ook nie so kieskeurig nie.
Jy moet tog ééndag sterwe.

Verwekker van malaria,
Sing maar jou laaste aria –
Nog een minuut vir grasie.
Al soebat jy nou nòg so lang,
Al sê jy ook: ek is nie bang,
Nooit sien jy weer jou nasie...

Hoe sedig sit hy, o die kreng!
Sy kinders kan maar kranse breng,
Nòu gaan die vabond sterwe...
Pardoef! Dis mis! daar gaan hy weer!
Maar dóód sal hy, sowaar ek sweer –
My naam is van der Merwe.

I had my moments in Tlhokomelo Higher Primary School because just like in Moruta Thuto, I was loved by many teachers. I was also liked by my fellow learners because I used to help them a lot with their school work. I would not call myself one of those intelligent children, all I did was work hard. I am one of those people who sets his mind on something and ensures that I complete it to the end.

The one moment that stands out in my life was when I was doing my Standard 4 which became a lesson for me. I think this is the moment in my life that I value the most because I owe my success in my career to this period. Every time I look back to this moment, my eyes fill up with tears and sometimes I choke with emotion. That moment shaped my schooling journey because of the lesson I learnt from the incident that took place.

I think it was a Tuesday when I became sick. My parents had to leave early because they could not afford much and relied on public transport to get to work. They had to take the train and that meant waking up early in the morning so that they were at the train station before 5.30 am to avoid being late for work. I have a younger sister who was still too young to attend school at the time. We did not have childminders or crèche facilities back in the day. We relied on a woman who stayed at a house on the corner of our street, to look after children in our neighbourhood. She was known as MmaTebogo (God Rest Her Soul) and she was a mother to a friend of mine that I grew up with. She was well known in our street and lived only four houses from ours. She used to charge a small fee to look after children in our street. So, every morning on our way to school we would drop my sister off at her place and pick her up when we returned.

On this particular day, I was sick with flu. I must say that I am one of those children who grew up sickly because I have a number of allergies ranging from certain food stuff to atmospheric allergens like pollen. I also have a problem with my sinuses and they used to bother me a lot back in the day. This was before I knew that you can surgically remove them. But I never removed mine and I still have them but I control them by taking medication daily. So you can imagine for yourself, suffering from all this and then suffering from flu at the same time. I had a terrible headache and could not breathe properly because my nose was blocked. I decided to stay home and my parents did not know that. I could not even call them to tell them because cell phones were not even in existence in Mzansi at that time. Now, this meant that my little sister could stay home with me and I had to look after her. I slept for most of the day as my whole body was aching.

When my mother got back home from work, she asked my little sister how it was during the day and whether she enjoyed the day at MmaTebogo's, as she was passionately known (God rest her soul). We all know that children do not lie and so she told it like it was. "Mom, I was not with MmaTebogo but I stayed home with big brother," she said. My mother was very upset with me and did not wait for my explanation, instead she told my father that I bunked school for nothing. Before I could explain, my father started shouting at me for bunking school. Normally, my father is the quiet one but he just had to raise his voice that day. He then ordered me to go and wait for him at the back of the house. I did as I was told. He then held me and made me bend forward with my head between his legs. He beat me so hard and I cried until I couldn't cry anymore. Normally my mother was the one who gave punishment but this time the tables were turned and my father took over. My father never gave a hiding to anyone in the house. This was his first hiding he gave to his children and certainly the last as well. From that day onwards, I vowed to myself that my parents would never have to give me a hiding because of bunking school. I promised myself that I would go to school no matter what the circumstances were. Part of it was my determination not to disappoint my parents again and the other part was just out of anger because I got a hiding even though I was genuinely sick. My mother decided to come to my rescue because she could see how my father was beating me and because she was feeling pity for me. After I got my hiding and had recovered from the crying, I then told my mother that I did not bunk school on purpose but that I was genuinely sick. She put her hand on the forehead and discovered that I had a high temperature. Knowing that I was a sickly child the two of them decided to take me to the family doctor in Zone 10 Meadowlands. It was not far from our house so the three of us walked there.

The doctor examined me and found that I had swollen tonsils and that indeed I presented with signs and symptoms of flu. He also checked my temperature, which normally goes up when you have an infection, and found that it is above the norm. Dr Ngwasheni booked me off sick for the remainder of the school week, meaning from Wednesday to Friday I was not to go to school. I was very distraught by this and decided I was going to spite my parents. They apologised all the way home and my father tried bribing me by buying me nice stuff at the shop. I got home, got into bed and slept. I didn't even eat, that's how angry I was at my parents. They told me that I should not go to school as per the doctor's instructions. The following morning when my parents were gone, I woke up and washed and off to school I went. When my parents came back home, they asked Jennifer, my little sister, if she enjoyed spending the day with me. She simply replied that I was not around as I was at school. My mother called me and shouted at me for going to school while I was booked off sick. My reply to her and my father was that I was afraid of the beating my father gave me thus I decided to go to school. The next thing I know tears were rolling down my cheeks and even though I had forgiven my parents, I never forgot the beating I received from my father the previous day.

My parents insisted that I stay home the following day but you know as a kid, you become very scared that history might repeat itself. So, I decided to go to school the following day again. I think my parents gave up on that and just let me be.

That week was the one that changed my life forever because I pledged to myself never to be absent from school ever again. I finished my schooling at Tlhokomelo Higher Primary School and went to secondary school. I started my years of schooling there in 1985 and in 1986, the Soweto riots began. There was a lot of *toyi-toying* going on and we used to burn tyres in the streets to create barricades so that cars that belonged to White businesses would be stopped and burned down. We used to take the drivers out of their cars, beat them up and chase them down the streets.

When all this happened we used to join in and help out in the name of the struggle but we never forgot our goal. I had six friends with whom we shared common goals and interests. We had one common goal and that was to study and complete school so that we could go to university and study further in our different fields. The friends that I used to share my secondary school days with are Joel Phatsoane, Phanuel Rapule, Happy Tshwene Mashiane, Pule Jacob Mnguni, Lemi Pascal Mataboge and the late Reuben Modise Mompati (God rest his soul). Modise went to study and worked as a teacher briefly before he passed away. Phanuel Rapule is studying at UNISA and continuing his law degree. Happy Mashiane studied lithography and used to work for UNISA as a printer. Joel Phatsoane also ventured out and worked for one of the private companies. I am not sure what he was doing there. Pule Mnguni is working as a law enforcement officer because he decided to go and study law enforcement and

Lemi Mataboge went on to study management and HR-related courses and owned a company with a colleague doing verifications and recruiting. At least none of us turned out to be a nobody and we have to thank being disciplined and the guidance from our beloved teachers because that's what got us to where we are.

We used to go to the laboratory and lock ourselves inside and study. Then, we would choose one of the team members to lead the discussions, especially those who were very strong in specific subjects. Each one of us was a subject specialist in a way because we had more knowledge of one or two subjects. When there was *toyi-toyi* for the pass-one pass-all, the Bantu education system granted us that. I guess they did not care whether we received the knowledge or not. I somehow want to believe that the apartheid government allowed us to attend schools because in that way they could keep track of what we were doing and it would keep us out of mischief and avoid going to the *mzabalazo* gatherings. They did not care what happened to us when we completed school because they knew that once we got into trouble, we would be locked up. That's how powerful the then government system was. So, the clan and I managed to stay out of trouble most of the time. We joined the group and took part in the *toyi-toying* until everyone got tired and went home. After that, we would go and study. So yes, we were much a part of the struggle as much as we were focusing on our studies. We did not want to be left behind with any of the two because they were equally important during our apartheid struggle times. School was going to open doors for us and, on the other hand, the struggle fed us with much-needed valuable information about the direction the country was taking, so we kept ourselves abreast of the developments.

We went through all the standards (currently called grades) flawlessly and all of us passed. No one was left behind until we entered the matric class door. One struggle we had to face during our schooling years was choosing which subjects we wanted to take to get accepted to university. This happened to us when we were doing Standard 8. I remember some of us chose the maths and science subjects route but we were chased out of those classes because the teachers told us that the classes were full. This is where the biggest challenge started and we were forced to take subjects that we never even wanted to do. And because that was how the Bantu education system was structured, we had to take what was imposed on us at the time or else face the challenge of not having a class to attend. This would simply mean that one would need to stay at home. We chose what was given to us. The subjects were English, Afrikaans, Tswana, History, Biology and Woodwork (which incorporated Technical Drawing). With these imposed subjects, we had no choice but to make sure that we passed and got out of that school and earned ourselves opportunities to study at tertiary level. We worked very hard and stayed together as the same group. We went through the standards without fail until we reached matric (now called Grade 12). I remember we started to cross-night just after receiving our books in February. For those who might not know, to cross-night in our days, was to study through the night until dawn. We used to get together around 7 pm to start studying. I left home around 6 pm so that I got there on time because I had the longest stretch to walk amongst all my friends as they stayed in and around Zone 3 which was not a far walk for them. We approached the principal and the caretaker of Tumang Primary School in Zone 3 Meadowlands. The principal gave us permission to utilise one of the classes for our cross-night studies on condition that we left the class clean. We made sure that we got all the necessities that we were going to need for the study group. We got ourselves a box of chalk, chalkboard duster and paper to write on. We then clubbed together to buy coffee, milk, sugar, tea, bread, butter, peanut butter and jam to keep us going through the night. One of us brought a kettle and each had to bring a mug and a spoon. These were the basics we could afford at that time because we were just learners and depended on our parents to give us money to buy them.

Knowing how the apartheid system ensured that our parents were earning a salary to just survive, this had an impact on how much they could afford to give me. At times, I had to use my lunch money to contribute to buying the basic items we needed for the study group. Despite all of this, I never gave up and carried on because I knew exactly what I wanted to achieve in life. My aim was to become an architect and an interior designer because I was very passionate and good in technical and art drawing. I grew up learning how to draw from my father as he was an artist himself. I used to sit next him and watch how he did his drawings and learnt from that. I had a passion for drawing and as a result, I ended up doing Technical Drawing in matric. I excelled in the subject achieving between 90–100% in the subject. As a result, the teacher asked me to help those learners who were struggling in the subject. I then went on to finish my matric and passed with an exemption D mark. I was the only one in our class to achieve that and one of six learners who obtained an exemption pass among the six matric classes that we had at the time. This was a great achievement at that time given the circumstances under which we were attending school.

This is the time when I realised the fruits of all the sleep-less nights that I had to endure during the year. My friends also passed their matric, but in respect for their privacy, I will not disclose the marks they had obtained. We were jubilant when we went to collect our matric results because despite all the challenges we faced, we had pulled through no matter what. The rioting had messed up the schooling system and most of the learners felt that it was rather useless to attend school. On the other hand, we saw it as a golden opportunity to keep studying regardless of the hardships and the end results were rewarding. I remember that we also used to attend extra classes at Wits University on Saturdays. We had to leave home in the early hours of the morning and only returned home late in the afternoon. We would sometimes come home around 5 or 6 pm. I lived the furthest away among the group and because of that I had to walk to Zone 3 to meet the rest of the guys so that we could walk to the closest train station, which was Phomolong to catch a train to Braamfontein where the campus was. Then we would walk from the train station to campus. This was something that we did every Saturday morning and late afternoon and it was a trip we enjoyed very much. I also took up extra classes in art and enjoyed every moment of it. These extra classes helped us pave our way to completing our matric. The lectures that we received there sharpened our minds and helped us cope with matric as we were receiving very minimal lecturing with all that was going on around us. We met very good people there who were always willing to share information with us that came in handy when preparing for the exams. I remember at one stage, our biology teacher taught us wrong things and we argued with her on that by correcting it because we had so much information that we'd been fed from attending at the university. Instead of embracing the inputs that we gave and correcting herself, she left the class and went and reported to the principal that we were challenging and embarrassing her. In any learning environment, we exchange information and learn from one another but the teacher didn't share the same sentiments because of how she handled the challenge by the learners. We ended up being summoned to the principal's office for challenging the teacher but that did not deter us. Instead we stuck to what we learnt and this helped us pass our matric.

02 Journey After High School: The Dream that was Never to Be

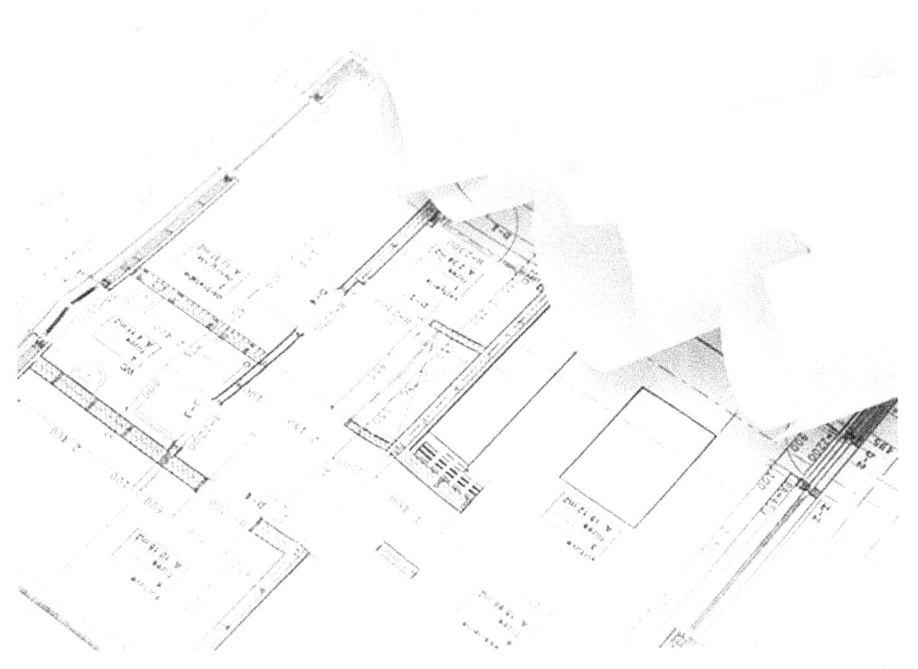

I must say that this journey is rather a very short one with very little to really talk about. What I can tell you is that my former teacher, Mr Mmoloke (God rest his soul) advised me that I should take up architecture as a career because I would do well in that field and make a good career out of it. Hence I thought about giving it a try and see where it would get me. I applied to several universities and had different challenges from each one of them. The first one was the University of Durban-Westville which declined my application as they only offered the course in Afrikaans and as we all know the apartheid era was responsible for this as this course was regarded as a Whites-only course. The second university that I applied to was the University of Cape Town. I had a very interesting challenge with this particular university. When I first applied, my application was accepted, however, the challenge was getting accommodation. The accommodation office called me to tell me that there were no rooms available, however, this was not the case. I found out later that rooms were indeed available but they were reserved for White students only. I then offered to look for accommodation closer to the university and I was told that it was not possible as it was a requirement that one stays on campus for reasons undisclosed to me. If you ask me, this was just a deterrent for me to be declined admission to the course. It is for this reason that my application was turned down. The irony of this was that when I applied the following year, I applied for admission, accommodation and a bursary. I was awarded the bursary and allocated a room but was not admitted to the university. This meant that all efforts were in vain because I was not going to be able to study what I so much wanted to study. Remember earlier on I stated that I was good at technical drawing. Now, this is where it came in. I enrolled to study architecture at these universities.

I then applied to the University of Witwatersrand and the University of Pretoria. They both told me outright that the course was meant for Whites only and no Black person had ever done the course. They further stated that even if they admitted me for the course, I would never make it as it was presented in Afrikaans. I then tried the University of Bophuthatswana and the response I got from them was that they did not take applicants from Soweto as students from there were always protesting and this would be a bad influence on students from Bophuthatswana. We have to remember that Bophuthatswana was an independent state at that time, so they had every right to make whatever decision as to who came to their state or not. I then tried Durban Technikon (which is now known as Durban University of Technology) and I still failed as I never received any funding and thus it was going to be difficult to even start with the course. I gave up on the dream in 1991 after a series of failed applications which made it clear to me that I would not be able to make my dream come true because of the situation in our country at that time. I opted to apply at INTEC College to undertake studies and was discouraged by various people stating that the course was not yet recognised and thus I would have difficulty obtaining employment. As we all know, we study so that we can get employment in order to live a better life. This was going to be fruitless and hence I finally abandoned the dream and threw in the towel. This struggle meant the end of my dreams of being an architect and I had to spend all of 1991 at home doing nothing and be like most of the guys who would *blom* (hang around) at the shops and corners. For the most part, I kept myself busy playing soccer, volleyball, tennis and also building cars out of wire and making go-karts out of wood. I remember sitting one day and thinking how I could make the go-kart safe. I then came up with a contraption to have a braking system. I managed to get a hand-brake from a scrapped vehicle and took a bicycle brake cable and attached it to the centre of a piece of a plank that I had placed behind the wheels. The piece of plank had rubber soles at each end that would come into contact with the rubber wheels. How it worked is that when you pull on the hand-brake, the cable would pull the wood forward and apply pressure against the rear wheels and the go-cart would brake. It was a process of trial and error. I had tried many times without success. Eventually, I managed to get it right and my go-kart had a braking system. Most of my friends copied what I had done but they also had to go through trial and error before they could get it right. I was an inventor of some sort hence it was never difficult for me to do the psychometric test because I enjoyed doing puzzles. I should mention that I was also good at making make-shift guitars and a lot of guys would come to me to learn how to make all these things. I guess I have a creative bone in me because even to this age, I still come up with creative ways to sort out challenges in anything that I come across. I never let up on a problem without finding a solution in the end.

Beginning of the Journey in the Military

Later in 1991, I saw an advert from the South African Defence Force (SADF) which is now known as the South African National Defence Force (SANDF), looking for volunteers who wished to take up a career in medical services. I must say that I did not know that I was actually applying to join the military. All I knew was that I was going to join the medical field but not in the military because the advert stated that they needed people to join the South African Medical Service (SAMS). I filled in the application and sent it via post the following day. I never really expected anything out of this. To my surprise, on 18 January 1992 I was called and told to report to Pretoria Station on 24 January at 8 am. I told my family about this and everyone was excited but I was scared because this meant a new life in a totally new and unfamiliar environment. The SAMS gave us a list of items we were required to bring with us. My family helped me prepare for my trip to Pretoria. This was a totally new ball game for me as I have never been outside Johannesburg let alone Soweto. This was very scary for me and to think that I was going to join the army as well exacerbated the situation. The day came and my bags were packed and I was ready for the road. My father took me to the taxi rank in town where I boarded a taxi to Pretoria. Fortunately, there were other people in the taxi who were going where I was going. We started talking about our new experience and this helped to minimise the fear and the anxiety I was experiencing. We finally reached Pretoria Station and we were met by men in uniform who started shouting at us the minute we got to the army trucks that were waiting to transport us to the military base. This put the fear back into me because I was not used to anyone shouting at me, let alone being in the military. We were transported to the military base where we were inducted and admitted as members of the Military Voluntary Service. We were the second intake of Blacks; the first was in June 1991. We were taken through the basic training programme where we were taught basic military culture. This continued until the instructors were happy that we could carry on with other training. We then graduated in the Basic Military Health Training which is equivalent to the Basic Ambulance Assistant course. This was done in a week and the lectures were offered in Afrikaans only. What helped me was the fact that I had an Afrikaans background and thus could grasp some of the medical terminology. We then finished the course and were given training in the Operational Medics Course which was the equivalent of the Ambulance Emergency Assistant course. We did this over the course of a month which was divided into two weeks of theory and one-and-a-half weeks of practical training. We did our practical training at Sebokeng hospital. We were fortunate as Sebokeng was one of the most busiest hospitals during that period because of all the riots that were taking place then. We got a lot of exposure over the short period that we did the practical training.

When we returned we were given driver training and taught how to drive military vehicles. This training was done so that we could obtain a driver's licence. We were then given military driver's licences which were only applicable to driving military vehicles. After training was completed, our group was then ready to be deployed to various regions in the country to start working. I was selected among the top five students to become instructors in the Medical School of the South African Military Health Training. My responsibilities included training members of the force and ensuring that their well-being was looked after. I was then afforded the opportunity to undergo a First Aid Instructors course that was offered by the First Aid League, which was offered to make us ready to become lecturers in the field. Once more their lectures were in Afrikaans and this posed another challenge but I managed to pass the course and it was broken down into 80% practical and 20% theory. After completion of this training, I was then required to lecture students who got into the system to do military service. They ranged from volunteers, nurses and the compulsory military service candidates that were mostly Afrikaners. It was difficult at first because I was never exposed to public speaking and thus had stage fright. When I started out I had to read straight out of the book during the first few lectures that I conducted. I gained confidence after training the third group of students that went through me. I then developed a method of going through the work, wherein I summarised the work on flash cards and did my lectures from there. I would stand in front of the class and read from the flash cards to remind me of what I needed to talk about next. This helped me tremendously as I gained confidence and the skills to present. I did this in such a way that one would not notice that I was reading from a reference. Over time, I started gaining popularity and more confidence as well.

I then went on to do various training courses which included the Operational Emergency Care Operations retraining course, the AIDS Train the Trainer course and the Emergency Care Instructor's course which gave more speciality in pharmacology, emergency Care and primary health care. I also completed the Regional Disaster Response and Trauma System Management training that was offered by the United States Air Force. It was during the time when I was still in the military, that I got an opportunity to go and study the much sought-after Critical Care Assistant course at a private emergency care training college. During those years, only the bravest of the brave and the right skin colour would qualify for this course. This course had very few, and I mean very few Black candidates attending it, so you can imagine for yourself what journey I was about to embark on. However, I never let any obstacle stand in my way, that's how determined I was.

04

The Advanced Life Support Training

The SAMHS had an agreement with Criticare Training College to send people like myself to attend the course and acquire the necessary skills. Back in the day, the course was a well sought-after qualification because not everybody could study such a course. I was afforded the opportunity to attend the Critical Care Assistant course at the Criticare College in Parktown in 1997 and the reason for that is that I had the passion and the drive hence I was selected. The ratio of Whites to Blacks was 9:1 but this should not be surprising because this course was mainly meant for White males; there were not even many White females in the profession at that time. In fact, one could count them in one hand. I was the only Black student in the class and I had it tough because some of the students did not like me and did not hide it. It was so bad that White students would receive a scope of the next test and I was left out. White students would go and gather in a pub across the street from the college after hours. They would wait for me to go to my room at Johannesburg General Hospital (now known as Charlotte Maxeke Academic Hospital) so that they could remain and receive the scope. This gave them an added advantage because they had information on what to expect in the test beforehand. I, on the other hand, had to study all the work that we did for the week and as we know, time was not enough to cover everything as there were other things to do besides studying. I carried on amidst the difficulty until I qualified to write the midterm exams before going on to the practical phase. This was done at various hospitals and on the road with instructors using emergency response vehicles (ERVs). I could not attend some of the practical shifts as per the roster as I had challenges with transport. As a result, I didn't qualify to write the final exams. The rules were very stringent back then. If, you missed one shift you were out because there was little to no time for one to work back missed shifts because it would've meant that they must set aside an instructor and a vehicle to work with. This proved to be impossible hence I dropped out of the course. However, there were other politics within the training academy that added to the pressure and prevented me from completing the course.

I was forced to return to my unit in Pretoria and continue doing my day-to-day work. This reflected badly on me. Some of my colleagues made fun of me calling me names. Some said that I thought I was better than everyone and who did I think I was to attempt to complete a course that was meant for Whites only. I was scorned at and as such, this made my life difficult on a daily basis. Still, I had told myself that I was not going to give up as I needed to prove to myself that I could make it. I was afforded an opportunity to attend the road practical and 10 shifts were allocated to me to complete this and qualify to write the final exam. I did not make it again because of the supervisor that I had at the time. He was very strict and told me that I should complete the course outside of working hours. I remember I scheduled some shifts and discussed it with him and even gave him the roster to which he agreed. So, based on our agreement I scheduled to work shifts with the EMS college. I remember I went out on a call to attend to a convulsing patient. While I was busy attending to the patient, I received a call on my mobile phone. My supervisor wanted to know where I was. This came as a shock to me because I had given him the roster beforehand and he should've known my whereabouts. He then insisted that I drop what I was doing and come back to the office immediately. I tried explaining to him that I was attending to an emergency, but he refused to listen. He told me he didn't care and that I should come back to the office immediately. His exact words were, "*Jy moet jou gat by die kantoor bring.*" Loosely translated this means, "Get your ass to the office." I just felt that the world was standing between me and my success. However, I obliged immediately after dropping the patient off at the hospital. As I entered his office, he started shouting at me at the top of his voice and asking me why I did not inform him that I was going for practical training. I responded that I had thought that since we had discussed this and I had given him the roster, I didn't think it would be a problem. Out of anger, he told me that the arrangement was now null and void and I could no longer go and do those practicals during working hours. Unfortunately, I had to comply because he was my superior and I could not argue with his instructions. This made it difficult for me as some of the shifts could only be done during working hours as they were scheduled during that time. This meant that once again, I could not write the final exams as I did not meet the requirements. I looked at my dream slip through my fingers but one thing I told myself was to never give up.

It was at this point when I felt like the whole world was against me and I felt like giving up altogether and remain an Ambulance Emergency Assistant. However, my hopes were revived when the Ambulance Training College had an agreement with the SANDF to train their members for free in exchange for assistance during exam times. I was among the candidates who applied to write the entrance exam and was accepted to the course. I attended the course and once more, there were only four Blacks amongst a group of 24 in the class. I must mention that I got accepted after the third attempt at the entrance exams. The first and second time I went, I was accepted but my supervisor refused to release me to attend. Now, need I remind you that the course once more favoured Whites and this was in 2001, seven years after the dawn of democracy in our country. As if I had challenges, the first time around when I attended the course at Criticare, well, my problems were far from over. I remember at times in the class we would be punished for not knowing how to apply theory in the practical environment. This was mainly because there was so much work to learn which consisted of anatomy and physiology, emergency care and pharmacology, which were at a higher level than AEA. So, I then decided to ask my supervisors at work to use the Simulation Laboratory after hours to practise our emergency care protocols and apply pharmacology accordingly. We went there almost every evening to practise. It was just me and my three Black classmates. Amazingly enough, this got us into trouble. I remember one afternoon the lecturer had us practising patient simulation in the classroom. Me and my partner were the first to go. He gave us a scenario and expected us to treat the patient according to the related protocol. We went down and started the simulation and did it outstandingly. He kept on changing the patient's condition in an attempt to catch us out but each time we would get it right and he was impressed. The other two Black students followed after us and they too got things right. The next to follow were two White students and one of them was the best performer when it came to theory. They started out okay but ended up fumbling along the way. The instructor became upset because this was embarrassing according to him. He even mentioned to them that they cannot be outsmarted by Black students. The whole class got punished for the rest of the afternoon and made to run as far as Lotus Gardens, which is an area a few kilometres from the college, and back to the college. As if that was not enough, he made us run around the perimeters of the hospital and that yard is very big. He only let us go when the day came to an end because he could not keep us after college hours.

We finished the theory phase and we all aced the mid-term exams and qualified to go on to the practical phase. I think this is the time when my woes started. I was arrested for contempt of court as I had breached the terms of a protection order. How this came about is that I was involved with a lady who was staying with me at the time. The intensity of the course meant that I had very little time for her and this made her upset and she decided to leave me. She left at a time when I was busy with the practical phase of the course. The fortunate part is that this was the hospital block so it was easy to catch up with all the missed shifts. The long and short of this story is that she was staying in town. She got her own flat and she had left some of her items at my house and so every time I went to town I would take these items to her flat. One Saturday, I was going shopping in Menlyn when I came across some of her stuff. As per the norm, I took them with to drop them off on my way to the mall. I got there and didn't know that she had company. When she opened the door, she discovered that it was me and became very upset and fought with me asking me why I had shown up without letting her know. I was perplexed because I had done this before and she didn't have issues and now all of a sudden she had a problem. In actual fact on one occasion, she invited me in and one thing led to another and the rest is history, I am sure you get the gist. Nonetheless, I gave her the stuff and made my way to the mall. A week went by and on the following Thursday around noon I received a call from Sunnyside Police Station. The person on the line asked me to come to the police station as there was a matter he wished to discuss with me. I went there not knowing that I would be placed under arrest for contempt of court. I was detained and taken to Kgosi Mampuru C-Max prison. I was there for a week before I appeared in court for a bail application. According to the law I was supposed to have appeared in court the day after my arrest but I was never brought before the magistrate because according to one police officer, they were trying to teach me a lesson by keeping me there for the whole seven days. Fortunately for me I had informed my lecturers about the incident and was allowed to work back the shifts that I missed, when I was released.

As if that was the last incident, I was in for yet another surprise. During one of the road practicals, we drove to Hillbrow to attend to a pedestrian accident that had taken place on a busy street. Under normal circumstances we were paired as students when we carried out our practical training so that one partner helps the other when they take the lead on a call out. It is a system that works very well in the ambulance services because the lead student has an extra pair of hands to assist. This is not only limited to hands but also extra eyes, knowledge and skills because students tend to help one another just in case one gets stuck on what to do next. There is always a synergy between the two students and this helps to make learning pleasant and also works to achieve goals.

On that particular call, we stopped in Louis Botha Avenue, one of the busiest streets in Hillbrow. We had to attend to a pedestrian vehicle accident (PVA) and the patient was lying across the double carriageway, direction South. The fortunate part is that he was not lying over on the other side of the road flowing in a northern direction. Now as training would have it, we were required to ensure safety in all aspects of the patient management process. We had to make sure that we were safe as students and that the patient was also safe. We also had to make sure that the accident scene was safe, meaning we had to secure it by laying out traffic cones to divert traffic away from the accident scene. We used to take turns being the lead student and, on this call, I was the lead student. I asked my lecturers to assist with securing the scene. Mind you, this was after they had told us while we were driving there that we must make sure that we use them to assist with scene safety and not leave them to linger around. I then thought to myself that this was now the opportunity to ask them to assist because my partner and I were going to be hands-on with the patient as he was critical and needed immediate medical intervention. We needed to ensure that the patient would not suffer further injuries.

I approached the lecturers and asked for assistance to secure the scene. I then went back to treating the patient thinking that they heard me and would do as I had requested. My partner and I were busy giving medical treatment to the patient and making sure that he was ready to be transported to the hospital when the ambulance arrived. All was going well until I felt a heavy whisk of wind going past me from behind. I lifted my head to see what it was. I realised that a bus had just gone past a few centimetres away from the soles of my feet. Now in our business that is a very risky situation, because paramedics sometimes end up being patients themselves (if they are not killed). This would've meant that the patient is left alone while the paramedic gets treated and this further puts the patient at risk. I then looked around to see where the lecturers were and to ask them why they didn't do as they were requested. I saw them standing around chatting and laughing. I lost my patience and approached them to give them a piece of my mind. I told them they had put us and the patient at risk by failing to do what they were asked to do. Instead, they were standing around and chatting. That was my biggest mistake. The lecturers didn't address me then. They waited for the patient to be loaded into the ambulance and transported to the hospital. I must admit these guys were extremely patient. They waited outside the hospital for us to clean the equipment and load it into the vehicle. They then decided that the night was over and we were now driving from Parktown to Pretoria. For those who know the area will know that you can cover that distance in under 45 minutes. However, for my partner and I, that was the longest drive ever. The lecturers gave us a tongue-lashing from all sides and we were never even given a chance to speak. The lead lecturer was driving at 60km/h. When we got to Pretoria, they kept us in the vehicle for another two hours lashing out at us without end. Now I am painting this picture for you so that you understand what I will be sharing with you later on. This will make sense to you once you marry the two and understand where everything emanated from. We went about our practical sessions and learnt quite a lot from the lecturers, hospital staff and other members in the emergency service environment. This helped us put everything into perspective and we were able to make sense of what we learnt during the theory phase.

The practical phase came to an end and we then went back to the college to start with debriefing of the practical phase of the course and to also commence with revision in preparation for the upcoming final exams. We went through the preparations seamlessly and were more confident because now we could marry the theory we had learnt in the first half of the year to the practical training we received in the second half of the year. The exams came and we sat and wrote. The exams were broken into four components: the theory exam which had two parts, short and long questions; the oral exams; the OSCE exams; and the patient simulation which was donc last. We went through all of the components of the exams and the one that scared us the most was the patient simulation because it was well-known that most students failed this component. This stood between you and completing the course. If you were not competent in this one aspect, you would have to redo the simulation exam. You would have to wait as long as six months to redo the exam when all the other students were doing their mid-year exams.

Well, I don't know whether I should say I was the fortunate or unfortunate student because I was the first to attempt the patient simulation exam. I must say I was very confident because I had put in the time and effort in preparation for this exam. I went through the patient simulation with ease and managed to treat the patient in an excellent manner. I completed the exam and was then instructed to sit in another class, away from all the other students who had not done the exam yet. This was to ensure that I didn't share information about the exam with other students. I sat there nervously waiting for the next student to join me. Soon, they came in one by one after completing a gruelling 20-minute simulation exam. We all finished and the lecturers left because it was lunch time. They told us they would share the final results with us after lunch.

We came back from lunch and waited in the classroom to hear our fate. A few minutes later, the coordinator came with the results sheet. They called out all the student's names in alphabetical order and gave them their results. I was last on the list. Twenty-three students passed all the components of the exams but I was not one of them. I was told that I did not make it because I had failed the patient simulation exam. I felt a cold chill going down my spine and thought to myself, *This cannot be true. This cannot be happening to me again. What have I done in this world to deserve this kind of punishment?* I actually became lightheaded from hearing the news. Remember, I had four failed attempts in the past due to matters beyond my control and this time I was certain that I was going to make it and finally become a paramedic, but all of this rested in the hands of two people. I enquired as to why I failed the patient simulation exam because I believed that I had done my level best in treating the patient according to scope of the treatment protocol. Mind you, there were students in class that I knew for a fact were not good enough and were struggling even though they tried their best. Well as fate would have it or should I say karma this time around, it was not to be. I was told that the external moderator was not happy with how I carried out the assessment of safety before I could start with patient management. He was very happy with the patient treatment part except that he was not happy with the safety aspect and as a result, I could not be considered competent. There were four examiners who all agreed that I performed excellently and could not fault me in any way but the moderator stood by his word and said he was not happy. I felt so helpless and hopeless but then quickly requested that the video recording of the exam be reviewed so that a decision could be made on this. The examiners and the moderator agreed and reviewed the video recording. They came back and the moderator still said he was not happy. The last option was to go to the principal of the college. Off they went to consult with the principal and they had the opportunity to view the video once more. That was the most gruelling wait I had to endure because my future was now in the hands of the moderator and the principal. As fate would have it, the results still came back negative because the principal was in agreement with the moderator, even though four of the six agreed that I did exceptionally well.

Now, rewind to the earlier incident that took place in Louis Botha Avenue. If you read the previous pages, you will remember what I said there. Now that incident came back to haunt me. Yes, the moderator and the principal were the same two lecturers that I shouted at and they felt embarrassed in front of their White counterparts. This was now payback time for me. They let my partner through because I was the one who left the patient and confronted them so I had to bear the brunt of that incident. They got me real good and this was a real and painful payback if I have to say so myself. One of the doctors came to me and asked me if I was privy to the patient simulation prior to the exam because I had done it so well. She said it was as if I was briefed beforehand on what to expect. She told me that no matter what they said or felt, the final decision lay with the principal and the moderator. I had to take it as a man and accept the fact that I was not going to graduate with my buddies because of this. All the other students passed; I was the only one who had failed. The pain that I felt cut very deep but because I was thirsty for this, I never gave up. I went back to the principal to enquire if there was a chance to undertake a remedial to which he responded that there was. He then briefed me on what I needed to do. To cut a long story short, in June 2001, I went back and did the patient simulation exam and this time I passed. This meant I had now finally qualified to be registered as a paramedic.

This was not the end of my struggles though because there were a lot of people who were not happy that I was now a qualified paramedic. I went back to work and continued doing my job as a lecturer but this time around I was a well-equipped and qualified lecturer. There were people who could not hide their unhappiness, but I didn't mind them and carried on doing what was expected of me. Remember my supervisor, who once called me to come back to the office, while I was busy treating an emergency patient? Well, of them all, he was one of the unhappiest. So, one morning after our tea break in August 2001, all instructors were expected to report to one of the classrooms and wait for the Officer Commanding (OC) to address us. We did as we were told. The next thing that happened, question papers were handed out to all of us. We were then told that we had to be prepared to treat patients at any time hence the mock exam without any preparation citing that when a patient collapses, we would not have the time to take out our books and review before commencing with treatment. I welcomed the approach because I was very confident when it came to the knowledge and experience I had acquired.

We wrote and the scripts were marked. I managed to obtain an 89% pass mark which I was impressed with. I later got to learn that the reason why this exam was conducted was that the OC wanted to check if I had obtained my qualification legitimately. That broke my heart because I had to go through the struggle to achieve my goal and even after attaining the qualification, I had to face critics who still did not believe that I had passed legitimately. I faced many more challenges before I decided to leave the service. I remember on several occasions I came up with suggestions to improve the learning environment at work, but most of the time my ideas were shot down. I was even told that it was not the civilian environment and that I should not come with a civilian mentality to the military. Mind you, I have been serving the defence force since 1992 so why should I be reminded about military principles? That tore me apart because I just felt that my worth was no longer recognised due to pure jealousy of my achievement. This reminded me of 1999 when I went to seek approval to go on the course. My OC told me straight that he didn't understand why I was wasting my time because according to him, I was clearly not going to make it. Indeed, I didn't get in during the selection process because someone had informed the college not to take me even though I was among the top 10 of all those who sat for the entrance examinations. This devastated me because I was so passionate and really wanted to do the course as it was going to open a lot of doors for me. I tried again in 2000 but without success. My Sergeant Major (God Rest His Soul) told me straight to my face that they would not release me for the course because they needed me in the training unit. And yet, they managed to release my White counterpart who went and attended the course for an entire year and yet did not make it. This was the most frustrating moment for me. My luck turned for the better in 2001 when the college requested the military to release me for the course. It was because they had seen my passion as I used to go and work with the college staff on the road during my spare time, just to keep myself updated with work.

Going back to describing my agony of working in the training college after achieving my qualification, I remember looking at the primary health care training manual. I found that it was a bit outdated and the quality was very poor. Also, because it was a copy of the original manual, it started to fade. I took it upon myself to renew the book as I typed it page by page and inserted new pictures and sketches, and also updated medication and protocols that were outdated and no longer in use, replacing them with the current medication and protocols. I put in a lot of work and even did research on what was current. I spoke to doctors and nurses at the hospitals to share with me what was current and I used that information to update the manuals. Boy, little did I know that I was inviting trouble for myself.

I went to present my work to the OC and his management team. You could see most of them were impressed with the manual and the changes. My OC was not impressed at all and told me where to get off. He asked me who permitted me to change military books. I tried explaining that I saw the quality of the previous book had faded but I was shot down like I had killed someone. "You do not have the right to change anything. 'Who do you think you are?' he said. I left the room more humiliated than I was more excited to have the opportunity to present my work.

Amazing enough, later on in the following weeks, one of the officers informed me that the OC took my work and went to present it as his own work to his principals. I was so shocked and disappointed that someone was now taking the glory for my hard work. That did not damper my spirit as I carried on working and improving myself and the lecture aids. I also rewrote the practical workbook for the students which they used to record their work when doing their practical training. At least that work was not shot down and it was because it didn't have to be presented to the OC. It was only presented to the wing commander. I was commended for my good work and going forward, that booklet was then used by students.

I was on a roll and I went on to prove myself when I was given the task of formulating course objectives for the Operation Emergency Care Practitioners. I did this alone and even presented the course in preparation for the final assessment by the regulating body, which was a requirement to enable our members to be registered on the board as they were not able to be registered before. The regulator created a register that registered military health practitioners. I was such a hard worker that the Officer Commanding awarded me a certificate of appreciation for my hard work and for going the extra mile. This proved that I was indeed serious about what I was doing. I went on to become the best instructor. I even managed to stand in front of the class and lecture without referring to a book or lecture notes as per requirements. This was already in my blood as I was very serious about this. I managed to produce average pass rates of between 92% and 98%. The students that I lectured came for retraining courses and others were first-timers on the course. The group that came for retraining ended up giving me the nickname "Professor" because they felt that I deserved the title. They attributed this to the confidence I had when lecturing them and the fact that they could ask me anything relating to the course and I answered them with ease.

I went along with this name and to this day I am still called 'Prof' (in short). This is indeed a privilege to be given a title even though in real life I am not a professor yet. I guess I went on to live up to the name as I can gladly and confidently say that I am well on the right path to becoming a professor. The other thing that encouraged me to pursue this is because I love studying and am very passionate about it. I am a hard worker in general and this is why I have managed to come this far. I went on to better myself in the defence force until I decided to resign in February 2003. I felt that I had had enough of the military and wanted to grow as an individual and also harness my skills and knowledge. My resignation was brought about by the fact that I was reporting to a person who was less qualified than I was in the medical field and thus, he stood in the way of change. Whenever I suggested a change to improve the methods in which we gave lectures, he would be against it because he had no clue what I was talking about. I tried going above him but also met resistance as the people above him were White and did not also understand why I wanted the changes. The other reason why they did this was to protect their fellow White colleague so that he did not appear to be incompetent. So I made a decision to leave and join an organisation where my skills and knowledge would be well received and appreciated.

I then joined the Tshwane Metropolitan Council as an operational paramedic. I joined them immediately after leaving the SANDF. This proved that people with my qualifications were much needed in the industry because it was a scarce skill. I operated around the Tshwane CBD, Centurion and surrounding areas. I sometimes used to cover areas in the north as well as Mamelodi and surrounding areas. At first, it was tough because I had to adapt to the ways in which things were done outside of the military as I was used to the command and control within the defence force. I had to learn and adapt quickly as well. The salary was much better than what the defence force was offering me at that time. I must say I did enjoy what I was doing as this came with an adrenaline rush as we dashed from one incident to the other and each day was different.

I did not stay that long with Tshwane Metro Municipality because I applied for a job in the North West Province Department of Health as a provincial programme manager for the Emergency Medical Services. I was the successful candidate amongst several other candidates that came for the interview. The irony of it all is that on the day of the interviews, I arrived early before everyone else. I even arrived before the staff who worked in the department arrived, I think it was around 07h15. The MEC (God Rest His Soul) was the first person to arrive with his staff. He greeted me and asked if I had been assisted. "No sir, I have not been assisted," I replied. He proceeded to ask what I was there for and I told him I came for an interview. He wished me luck and told me, "The earliest bird catches the fattest worm," and that he liked my work ethics and punctuality. Other candidates started arriving well after 8 am. Mind you, I had to wake up very early in the morning to drive to Mafikeng. I left my home in Pretoria at 3.30 am which simply meant I didn't sleep enough and still had a long trip to navigate. The funny story about this whole journey was that I was broke as a church mouse. If you think back, I was working in the military and our pay date was the 15th and now I joined Tshwane and their pay date was the 25th. The interviews were held around the 15th of the month and I didn't even have enough money to get to Mafikeng. I called people to lend me money and all of them told me one story after the other. I then decided to call my friend from school, Lemi, to ask him for money. I explained to him that I had to attend an interview in Mafikeng. He then told me to come to Soweto to fetch the money and lucky enough, the money I had on me was enough to get me to where he worked. I waited for him to knock off and we left for his house. He stopped by the filling station and filled the car with fuel and then proceeded to the ATM to withdraw money and he gave me R500. When we got to his place he asked me how I planned to get to Mafikeng and I was lost because I had never been there before. He then said to me that Mafikeng was far and I would arrive there late if I were to use public transport. He then said to me I should take his car and go for the interview and that I could return it when I came back. It was Tuesday and the interview was on a Thursday. Long story short, I went to Mafikeng with his car while he used taxis to go to work. As I mentioned earlier, I was the first to arrive but guess what? I was the very last person to be interviewed. My interview took place at 5.05 pm. I then had to drive back to Pretoria that same evening because I had nowhere to sleep. I arrived around 10 pm and called Lemi to tell him that I would bring the car to him the following day and amazing enough he didn't have a problem with that. I will never forget the selflessness of this brother of mine to sacrifice just so that I could go for an interview and arrive on time. He was more concerned about my wellbeing, comfort and safety, which I appreciated very much to this day. Every time I tell this story, my eyes well up with tears knowing that I have such a brother in my life.

05

The North West Department of Health

Journey with the DoH North West

joined the department in June 2003. It was scary and exciting at the same time. I was supposed to start on 1 June, however, the date fell on a Saturday which meant I could only assume duties on Monday, 3 June. The salary was much better than what I was paid in the defence force and Tshwane Metropolitan Municipality. I was earning three times the salary I was earning in the military. You should've seen my excitement when I got my first pay cheque. Joining the department was the moment of truth for me to prove to myself whether I would cope or not with the functions of the position which were way above what I was used to. It was a test as I had to get used to the working environment of the public sector because remember I came from the military where the system was autocratic. The commands were hardly challenged and we had very little say in the decision making. We were given instructions on what to do most of the time. Now, in the public sector it worked differently because as a manager in charge of operations in the service, you are required to make decisions that will take the service forward and in the best interest of the patient. I had to start getting used to the environment and its challenges. I coped very well as we took the service to greater heights. I had a very wonderful supervisor who guided me most of the time. That made my transition very smooth even though we had hiccups here and there.

The first six months on the job saw me coming up with positive changes and at the same time learning the ropes. I had to learn quickly and it was rather a tough journey especially having to transition from being a course coordinator and operational paramedic to being a programme manager, which were very big shoes to fill. I have, for some odd reason, managed to survive regardless of the tasks in front of me. This came at the time when EMS in the North West was still in its infancy stages as it had just recently been taken over from the District Municipality in 2001.

This meant that there were a lot of systems one had to put into place. My military skills and precision helped me a great deal because I did not struggle that much. The only battle I had was the language used. Military language is different from civilian language and having served for 11 years, one was drilled down to the last bit in the military. Now, I had to abandon that language and conform to the civilian way of speaking. I had to learn and I had to learn very fast. I did so and began to cope very well within the environment. I remember I was so much of a disciplinarian to the point that some of the managers and employees went to complain to my superiors that I was very hard on them. I was called to my principal's office and was given a pep talk. I was requested to reduce being strict. My boss said to me, "As much as I understand that you want to bring discipline in the service, you must also remember how the public sector functions. It is union-ised and the last thing you want to do is to alienate and antagonise them (the unions)." He advised me that I needed to adopt a stra-tegic approach when dealing with issues in order for me to get through to employees and the managers as well. That meant that I had to find a much more subtle way of instilling discipline instead of going the rigid military way. I did find a way because I know that once I had spoken things started happening and this meant that I was on the right path.

The changes we brought about as a team were quite signifi-cant and very visible, which meant that we were making good strides. This is one of those achievements that makes me smile when I look back to the contributions I made and changes to the North West Emergency Medical Services. It was a tough and challenging journey but I survived nonetheless, with the help of my manager/supervisor.

On the social side of my life, I didn't have much to do because Mafikeng is a very small place and thus did not have a lot of activities after hours. I then decided to go and find out from the University of North West which course I could enrol in. I was advised to go the Graduate School of Business and Government Leadership. There I was advised to enrol for the Post Graduate Diploma in Business Management. After the modules were read out to me, I felt that it was a step backwards for me. I made more enquiries and was told that I could also enrol for a Master in Business Management (MBA) if I was in possession of a diploma from any tertiary institution. Unfortunately, I did not have one. I then enquired if there were alternative ways to enter into the programme and I was advised that I should follow the RPL (Recognition of Prior Learning) process. The RPL plus work experience and position would play a role in the selection pro-cess. I was further advised to write a 10-page essay about why I wanted to do the MBA degree. I did that and as it turned out, I became one of the preferred candidates to be on the course. I was subjected to a psychometric test as well which I passed without a problem. What helped the most is the fact that I used to undergo a lot of psychometric tests in the military and so I was already familiar with the process. After successfully com-pleting all the processes, I was admitted to the MBA programme and was eligible to register in February 2004. I was very excited and looking forward to starting with my studies.

I was cautioned that not many students who do not have an Honours degree manage to complete the programme. This was due to the fact that they faced a challenge with research because they were not exposed to it prior to the Master's degree. I was scared and worried at the beginning because I knew I got myself in too deep. I didn't know what I was going to do or where to start, however, I undertook the journey regardless of the fear and the many doubts I had. I just told myself that I needed to work twice as hard to ensure that I grasp everything that I would be taught on the course and that I did.

06

The MBA Journey

enrolled in February 2004 and we were told we needed to attend the pre-MBA training course. This gave us an overview of the programme and also improved our skills in certain aspects. This was an exciting course as we learnt more about each other and more importantly, about ourselves. This helped us evaluate ourselves and what we are capable of in order to ascertain whether one is ready to walk this stressful MBA journey. The two modules I enjoyed were computer literacy and soft skills. I guess being self-taught in basic computer skills drew me into computer literacy and I enjoyed it. The soft-skills module was also close to my heart because it taught me the skills needed to deal with employees. I found myself excelling in this module even though I had never received prior training. I guess one could call it an inherent character. This is when I got to discover that I have empathy towards others, which can be a good or bad trait to have, especially when people take advantage of this.

When we finished the pre-MBA course we were then told that we were ready to start with the MBA programme. I must admit that it was difficult at first but nothing was going to discourage me from achieving my goal. I went on with the course with its hurdles but managed to carry on regardless. The one challenge was that I was never exposed to writing assignments of that magnitude or even do presentations at such a high level. After all, I did not have a degree to my name. This became a challenge that I vowed to tackle head-on and never allowed it to deter me from what I wanted to achieve.

I was very active in class because I wanted to learn more and this came in handy because I got more and more exposed to learning in such an environment. I remember the class chose a group of us to go and speak to management of the school and raise some of the concerns that we had. Because I was vocal and stood for what was right, I was then, by default, chosen as the class captain of the MBA class. My colleagues told me that I had the best interests of the class at heart. The second thing that put me on the map was that we were required to do presentations of the group assignments. There were seven of us in my group and we had to take turns during each session to do presentations. On one particular day, one of the ladies had to do a presentation on one of the modules. Mind you, we got marks based on how well our presentation went. In this instance, things were not going so well. I can tell you that if she had carried on we would have failed this presentation and obtained lower marks for this module. I could not let this to happen so I then jumped in to save the day. I took over the presentation and did a sterling job at it. I guess my military days' presentation skills came in handy because we did so well. I must also state that I didn't do this in a harsh manner, as the lecturers actually encouraged group members to actively participate when one of ours was on the platform. So, I did this to save the day and took over as if it was my turn to carry on. We ended up getting 92% for our presentation which was well deserved.

I made great strides and was able to hang in there until we wrote our exams. It was tough indeed but one became better with time as we navigated through the modules. The first year went very well. I passed the exams with ease. During this time I didn't spend much time with my family as I had to juggle between work, school and family time. I had worked on a schedule which allowed me to have a little bit of family time and still be able to study. I was in the office from 7.30 am to 4.30 pm. I would then go home and from 5 pm, I would spend time with my family and catch up with the kids. Then I would go to the study table and study from 8 pm to around 1 am. I maintained this routine and it seemed to work very well as I was able to cover most of the work throughout the year. That was the year that I came up with the

3D principle (dedication, discipline and determination). The 3D principle helped to keep me grounded as I lived according to that and never allowed anything to sway me from my studies. Some of my friends were not happy that I could no longer spend time with them. However, I told them that studies don't go on forever and that when I was done, I would spend time with them again. I passed my first year MBA modules and this was an achievement for me because I never believed that I could make it. I was ready to tackle the second year with more confidence acquired from the interactions and journey of the first year.

I started the second year in 2005 and was again chosen as class captain by the group because they said that I did a wonderful job during the first year. We went through the course until it was exam time. I had passed some the modules and also failed a few. This was attributed to the fact that my sister passed away before we sat for the final exams in the second year. I had to spend a week and a half at home ensuring that everything was in order and to bury my sister (May her soul rest in peace). I was very close with my sister and having to see her suffer through her illness and her subsequently passing on hit me very hard mentally. The week immediately after my sister's funeral was the start of the exams. I did not adequately prepare for it as I was busy with the funeral arrangements and the mental trauma just put me in a difficult state of mind. We wrote the exams and I failed some of the modules that I wrote immediately after the funeral, because I did not prepare enough for the modules.

I was fortunate to be given a second opportunity to sit for the exams and I passed those modules because this time I had enough time to prepare with nothing hindering me. I am a hard-working person and this assisted me in achieving my goals. I undertook research during the middle of the second year and my supervisor was Prof. Temane from the Potchefstroom

University. We had a wonderful relationship and hence we could do a lot as a team. My research was deemed to be very good and I was allowed to write it in a journal format instead of a full mini-dissertation. This meant that I wrote less than 40 pages when the mini-dissertation required more than 100 pages. I managed to complete my research and graduated with an MBA during the April 2007 graduation ceremony. I was elated but then I thought to myself, *What next?*

07

The Doctoral Journey

decided to enrol for the PhD programme which I started in July 2007. This was barely three months after I had graduated with an MBA and I had initially told myself that I was going to take a break for a year from studying and focus on other things. When I looked around me there was nothing much really to focus on except studying. I was allocated the same supervisor I had at MBA level. Things did not go well with the supervisor as the feedback was very slow, thus delaying progress. In November, after several failed attempts to get feedback from the supervisor, I went to complain to the graduate school to intervene in locating the supervisor. The graduate school failed and then decided to allocate me another supervisor. We started work at the beginning of December but had to cut it short because it was recess period. We commenced in February after the schools reopened. It must be noted that I was still working on my proposal at the time as the new supervisor had a different ideology and approach to the study that I was undertaking. I had to change a lot of things that were agreed upon with the previous supervisor even though we did not finish. This meant a lot of work and effort was wasted and thus work had to be embarked on. I did not mind this as I believed that she was an expert in the field and knew what she was doing. Besides this, we were advised never to stand up against supervisors or rub them up the wrong way because they can determine whether you progress or not. Besides all of this, I was a student who came to learn and had to listen to what my supervisor said.

We had many meetings while working on the proposal until it was ready for presentation in July 2008. I presented the proposal and it was conditionally accepted provided I made certain changes to it and submitted it to the research committee. I went ahead and made the changes and then sent them to my supervisor for endorsement and to write a confirmation letter that the changes has been effected as requested. I gave her the document in August 2008 and waited for her response. I never received any response and after making several enquiries, I went to the supervisor's office to try and find out what the problem was. This is where I learnt that all deans had a meeting with the rector and the rector advised the supervisors not to supervise students anymore as they had a lot of work to deal with. All this happened in October and that meant I wasted another three months. I then approached the director of the graduate school and he told me that he would make a plan and would come back to me as to who my new supervisor was going to be. Towards the end of November after numerous attempts to find out who my supervisor was, I was told that Prof. Maaga was my new supervisor and that I should contact him to secure an appointment with him. I must say I was excited to have to work with him because he taught us research methodology during the MBA course, and I loved how he approached research. I did so and we met and I gave him my changed proposal. He had a look at it and after two days he came back to me and told me that it was acceptable and I could submit it to the research committee. I did so and it was endorsed. This meant that I could advance to the next level of the research. I met with the supervisor and planned how I was going to structure the first two chapters of my research. It took me three days to complete chapter one and I submitted it to my new and progressive supervisor, who then endorsed it. It was now time to focus on chapter two. I had an advantage because I had already done 70% of the work during the time I was waiting for a new supervisor to be assigned to me. So, it took me about two weeks to complete chapter two and I submitted it to my supervisor. He endorsed it as well and told me I could move on to chapter three. I started chapter three which focused on research methodology and I completed it after several meetings with my supervisor and did all the changes he advised me to make. I submitted it to my supervisor in May and he was happy with the contents. I could not make a presentation at that time as the next colloquium was set for July 2009. I then managed to present chapter three in the July colloquium and it was conditionally accepted, subject to very minor changes, which made me so happy because it then meant that I was on the right path.

The highlight of the presentation was when I was done with my presentation, one of the White professors stood up and complimented my presentation. He said that since he had started attending colloquiums, mine was by far the best presentation he had listened to and that it was well structured and well presented with confidence as well. This made me feel very proud as I was starting to make a difference in my career. This also showed how much I had grown academically and it gave me more courage to carry on and want to do more. However, I faced a challenge in that I could not carry on with data collection because the Research Ethics Committee had met and returned my application as they needed clarity on a few issues. I completed the response and sent it back to them but had to wait at least eight months before I could get a response. This created a further delay in my progress as I now had to wait for the Ethics Committee to come back to me. I submitted my request for an ethical clearance certificate in 2008 and right up until the end of the year, I did not receive a response. This was required by the Department of Health and Social Development both in the North West and Gauteng before they could allow me to carry out data collection. This meant that I was further delayed by about nine months waiting for the Ethics Committee and the departments (Gauteng and North West) to come back to me so that I could start with data collection. I had then told myself that I was going to work right through the holiday season to ensure that I was on track otherwise this was going to delay my other study plans with UNISA. I had enrolled for a Master's in Public Health with UNISA and was accepted provided that I was in the final stages of my research. This meant that I was either at the level of data collection or had finished it in time to commence my studies at UNISA. Unfortunately, this never materialised because when it came to me starting with my MPH, I wasn't anywhere close to finishing my research.

In the meantime, I managed to get feedback from the provinces stating that I could go ahead and collect data within the respective EMS bases. I engaged with the managers of the bases and took the data collection tool (questionnaire) to them and explained to employees how it should be completed. I had to travel to various EMS bases within the North West and Gauteng provinces to ensure that the documents were delivered. In some instances, I had to sit while the participants completed the tools and handed them back to me. This was great because I could leave with the questionnaires knowing that they were fully completed instead of having to send them back to the respondents, because chances are they would never be returned or they would be incomplete, and I could not use them. This proved to be a success as I managed to collect 70 more questionnaires than what was planned for. It took me at least two weeks to complete the data collection process. After that, I faced another challenge. This time I had to find a data analyst who specialised in both statistics and social research. It was very difficult to find such a person and instead, I managed to find a statistician who claimed to have an understanding of completing data sorting and analysis. My supervisor and I met with him to explain what was expected of him and he mentioned that he understood what needed to be done. He requested a period of three months to complete the process and we gave him the three months to do his work but we were very disappointed when he came and presented what he had done. It was not according to our brief. The man seemed not to have understood what we requested of him in our briefing meeting. You can just say he worked but it was a matter of "garbage in, garbage out" as he did nothing different to what we had already done. I think he did not understand what was requested from him or this type of data was just above his level. Maybe he did not know how to carry out data analysis after all. He told us he was a statistician but had very little experience in doing such work. We chose to go with him because we could not find anyone to assist with the process as we were running out of time. Little did we know that we were actually going to waste more time with this gentleman. He worked for five months on the documents with no positive outcomes at all.

It was now 2010 and with all the hustle and bustle to sort out things and be ready for the start of the World Cup, pressure was mounting to complete the data analysis process. My supervisor suggested that we look for someone else. The search was daunting given the fact that we had a very limited pool of people to choose from who matched the criteria of a person who could carry out this type of data analysis. We were once more racing against time to find a person. We were then referred to yet another gentleman who had done a Master's degree and had a background in social research. He proved to be the best choice at the time. We engaged with him and explained the process and what we aimed to achieve out of the process. He understood and spoke the same language as us. This came as a relief because finally we found someone who understood what we wanted. We submitted all the documents to him in May 2010. He promised that it would take him three months to complete the process. This was the best news ever because it meant that I would be able to present my results in late 2011 after completing the whole research. The World Cup was around the corner and this meant that a lot of people were going to be busy, including myself because I had to be directly involved in the planning and execution of medical deployment of EMS personnel.

I requested to be transferred from North West to Gauteng because I felt redundant at work and was not doing much for most of the day. I wanted to join a department that was progressive – one that would challenge my ability so that I could learn and grow. I moved to Pretoria in June 2010 and started my job at the Gauteng Department of Health. It was in the same field I was serving in when I was in the North West. It was a big move for me because it meant I had to adjust my lifestyle when it came to work. I now had to travel for two hours to work compared to the 15 minutes that I used to drive when I was in the North West. This also meant that I would have to travel to Mafikeng for any contact sessions with my supervisor and it would require that I book for overnight stays and at times staying the whole weekend to avoid going back and forth when my assignment was due for submission. This was not easy on the family, especially my wife because it meant that I was leaving her behind with the kids. This was proving to be hectic considering that I had to work at three stadia during the World Cup games. On some occasions I would find myself working at three stadia on the same day just at different times. This was tough but I was equal to the task. During the World Cup no contact was made with the data analyst as it was hectic and one needed to focus on the task at hand. If you can remember very well, the World Cup started on 11 June 2010 with a match between South Africa and Mexico. It ended with a final match between the Netherlands and Spain on 11 July 2010. For those who may have forgotten, Spain were crowned champions. This now meant that it was back to business with the data analysis process as the World Cup tournament was behind us. We only made contact with the data analyst after the World Cup and he indicated that he hadn't started with the process as he had to travel out of the country during the World Cup season as he was requested to come home. He then promised to start with the work once he had settled in back at work upon his return from Ghana.

We gave him time to work on the information in the hope that something positive would come out of it. Time flew past very fast and we decided to make contact with him towards the end of November 2010 hoping that he would have some results. When we spoke to him, he indicated that he hadn't done anything yet because he was drowning in his own work and hadn't had the chance to even look at the information that we gave him. He requested that we give him time and he would get back to us with something positive. He made contact in mid-December and it was not good news. He mentioned that he still hadn't had a chance to start with the work and suggested that we look for another person to assist us. This was yet another blow because it meant that we had lost yet another year without any progress on our side. I agreed with my supervisor that we should start our search at the beginning of 2012. This was a devastating blow to the progress because it meant that we were back where we started. Mind you, the university only gives you five years to complete your PhD and this was approaching very fast. There was not much progress made with our data analysis and we still had so much work to do beyond that stage.

We began the search for a new data analyst in January 2012. We managed to get a few names from the graduate school. Some were willing to help while others declined outright stating that they had too much on their plate. We engaged with those who had agreed to assist, but they declined the minute they understood what we needed from them. At the end of the day, we came out with no one who was willing to assist us. Months went by and we were now in May and the distance between me and the supervisor was proving to work against us. We had to synch our schedules and find the right time to meet, which was not always the case. This was hindering progress so much and delayed us drastically. The search continued but to no avail. In September 2012 we approached the University Computer Science Faculty for them to load the SPSS software so that we could start with the data loading and cleaning in an effort to make work lighter for the person we might find to assist us with data analysis. They agreed and loaded the latest software for us and we started right away with the capturing. It was a daunting task because I had to capture over 570 documents that were six pages long. It took me three months to complete the process before I could take the completed work to my supervisor for verification. I only managed to take the information to the supervisor in November and he was happy with what I had done thus far. He then checked for errors and omissions to ensure that I did any corrections that were needed. There was constant back and forth communication between us and travelling to meet and go through the work. I had to work hard in the December period to ensure that my information was ready for January 2013.

We finally managed to complete the task at hand. We did the data analysis after a series of intense meetings and back and forth travelling. In March 2013, I was ready to make a presentation at the research colloquium. We sent a letter of intent to the university and they gave a positive response that we could come and make the presentation. In May I started my new job with the Mpumalanga Department of Health. This meant I was moving further away from Mafikeng. I was adding another 360km to the 340km that I was travelling when I was in Pretoria. This meant that I had to travel about 700km in and 700km out and this took its toll on me. The date of the research colloquium was set for May 2013 and I had to take time off to make the presentation yet I was still new in my office.

At the research colloquium we were 10 students who were waiting to present. There were five students who were doing a proposal defence presentation and four who were presenting their research methodology. I was the only one doing a presentation on the data analysis and results. However, this did not mean that I was only presenting on the data analysis. I had to do a presentation from the first chapter to the last. I had 35 slides in my presentation and the time that was allocated was 15 minutes for each student. Our supervisors were present to also assist us with responses where necessary. All other students presented and some of them made it to the next level while others did not. I was the last one to present and my turn came to do the presentation and I took everyone in the senate through a journey of my thesis. I was left with 10 slides when I was told that my time was up. I pleaded for more time, stating the reason that I was the only student who was required to present the entire thesis while other students were presenting only portions of their work. The committee agreed that it was an oversight on their part when they were allocating time to each student and didn't take that into consideration. The time keeper was then requested to add 10 more minutes to allow me to complete my presentation and to also allow time for questions and discussions. I did my presentation and completed it. At the end of the presentation, I was asked only three questions. Two of the questions were related to seeking clarity about questions in the manuscript that the committee members had not gone through yet. I pointed out to them where they could find the information and they were happy with the response. The third question was based on the last part of the research which the professor felt needed a little bit more information to give it more weight. We agreed to add more information. This was not a daunting task as the information was initially included but my supervisor asked me to remove it for fear of adding too much information. The final decision by the committee was that they were happy with the presentation and that I could submit my work for examination provided I made that one addition as pointed out by one of the professors. We went back and made those additions and got the document ready for submission after cleaning it up thoroughly and even after taking it through the language and grammar editing process, which I had to pay for.

The document went back and forth several times between myself and the examiners. What was frustrating was that the examiners were not consistent with their approach. They would make comments on the document as a first round of examining and suggest that the suggestions and comments be incorporated into the document. What was more frustrating was that after making those suggested changes and sending the document back, they would make additional comments. Two of the examiners made comments that meant that the document would have to be changed back to its original draft. This was disheartening because it was a waste of valuable time and meant more delays for me to graduate. What was even more puzzling was that the suggestions made by the examiners were conflicting in some instances. I then concluded that the examiners did not sit with the original document when they made comments to do a comparison. Otherwise they would be aware of what they suggested in the first round of submission. Mind you, with all of this, I had to print four copies, one for each examiner and the other copy for my supervisor. I then had to travel all the way from Nelspruit in Mpumalanga to Mafikeng in the North West to make my submission. The reason I did not use a courier service was that in the past I had submitted documents and only realised later that the university had not received the documents. So it was futile for me to use the courier service. I have always believed that when you want something done correctly, do it yourself to avoid disappointments and delays. Furthermore, all the printing was costly for me because it meant that I had to print 275 pages four times, which is a ream and a quarter and on top of that, I was using a lot of printer toner. I had to do this exercise four times. Eventually my supervisor then gave clarity on how to deal with them to ensure that we pick on the valuable comments and makes changes according to these. We eventually managed to make the changes and the document went back to the examiners, who finally approved the thesis for publication. But wait, there was another twist to all of this as if I hadn't had enough challenges already. I was told that the Dean secretly sent my document to a professor friend of hers in Australia to check its authenticity and the quality of the work. A reliable source informed me that when it came back, I was placed amongst the 15% top achievers in the university. This saw me being nominated to be a member of the Golden Key International Society, which recognises the 15% top achievers in an academic institution. Membership is by invitation only and not everyone can become a member. You have to be amongst the elite few to be chosen. This lifted my spirit because it simply meant that my thesis was of top class. This was the greatest news ever and I couldn't wait to share it with my family. This was a rare achievement and needed to be celebrated, however I did not have money to even have a small celebration because I was financially drained by all the travelling and printing.

This meant that I was ready to graduate after a very long struggle. At least all three examiners agreed that my thesis was good enough for publication. The graduate school called me and gave me guidelines on preparing the document for final approval, which I did and submitted. I was then required to print six leather bound copies that were to be submitted in order to be legible for graduation. I looked for a company in Johannesburg that did leather binding and had to pay for them to produce the documents. I then went and delivered the documents in person to ensure that the university received them. Mind you, the struggles that I have experienced and endured, have brought me to a point where I did not trust anyone and would rather see things through up to the point where they land in the right hands. I was pleased with the progress thus far and was ever ready to graduate.

Just when I thought my troubles were over, another problem cropped up. I was told that I owed the university about R56,000 in outstanding fees. I engaged the finance office to seek clarity and was informed that the outstanding amount was due to the fact that I had been paying less than what I was supposed to pay. I argued in my defence that it was not my fault as I paid according to the quotations that were given to me over the years. I even showed them proof of such information. This matter dragged on for a number of years before it was finalised. I went back and forth to the university to try and resolve the matter but without much success. I was on the verge of giving up but I then told myself that I had come so far and could not give up now. At the same time, there were other issues impacting me. I had people scolding me saying that I was lying when I said I was doing my PhD and that is why I had not graduated yet. This is what pushed me to fight so that I could clear my name and eventually get to graduate. A lot of people had doubts and called me a fake, which got to me somehow, but I was not about to give up.

The university took me to its lawyers for the collection of outstanding debt. This meant that the matter was to drag on longer because there was a misunderstanding between me and the debt collectors. I sent them all the correspondence that I had at my disposal trying to prove that I was not in the wrong. The White lady that was helping me there promised to look into the matter for me and even contact the university to get clarity. Remember, once an institution hands a matter to the debt collectors, they expect that debt collectors will handle it until all that is due is paid. The lady came back to me after several months and told me that the university is standing by its story that I owe that amount of money and I was liable to pay it. What brought about the dilemma was that at the beginning of each year during the registration period, I would go to the finance office and request for a fees quotation. The lady who worked in that office would only give me the registration fees which was exclusive of the course fees. Unknown to me, I took the quotation and applied for finance with Eduloan and paid the amount in full either on the same day or the day after, depending on when Eduloan would process the payment. Little did I know that I had course fees that were outstanding and according to the finance section, all of those amounts accumulated to the R56,000 that I owed. I mean I didn't work in the finance office to know what amount I needed to pay and I was dependent on the finance lady that assisted me.

The White lady working for the debt collection firm resigned without me knowing about it and several months went past. The year was over and I still did not have any clarity about the alleged debt I was told I owed. As each month of the year went past, I enquired with the university regarding my graduation and I was given the same response. I even called the debt collectors to find out if the matter had being resolved. I told them that whenever I called the university, they told me that I had to take up the matter with the debt collector as the matter was now with them. No one from the university's finance section was willing to help me. Four months into the year, a Black lady called me from the law firm and told me that she was assigned my case and had been instructed to collect money from me. I told her that the matter was still *subjudicé* because a White lady from the firm was busy handling it. She then informed me that the lady had since resigned and that there was no information on the system to show what she had done with the matter. This then meant that we needed to start from scratch. I sent her all the communique that I had between me and the White lady. She also promised to have a look into the matter but I guess it wasn't meant to be, because she never came back to me for several months. The year was almost at the end and graduation season had come and gone. This meant that I had to wait for the new year to start the process again and see where it led.

It was now the beginning of 2017 and I was more eager to fight this matter to ensure that I graduated. I called the law firm and was told that they would only be able to attend to my matter in February when the university opened because there was no one they could speak to at that moment. Another disappointment which came with another delay. In February I got in touch with them to find out what had been said and guess what? The person that was dealing with the matter from the university side had resigned and they were still waiting for someone from the university to give them feedback. The month of February went by and anxiety started setting in because I wanted the matter resolved so that I could graduate during the April graduation. As fate would have it, I was faced with yet another struggle that came with a lot of back and forth but no tangible outcome.

I then decided that this is enough and I drove to Mafikeng towards the end of March and I engaged the office of the rector to explain my dilemma to him. He then directed the finance office to look into the matter objectively and ensure that I was given the assistance that I required. After several consultations and consolidations, the finance office came back to me and agreed that they would reduce the amount to R26,000 since the fault was partly on their side for misleading me with the quotations. I was jubilant as I had saved up some money so that I could settle the debt. I then asked them to remove the matter from the debt collector's roll as well because I intended on settling the matter by paying directly into the university's account. I then rushed to the bank in Mega City to go and pay the R26,000 that I was told I owed. While I was waiting in line, I received a call from the university. The lady on the other end of the line asked me if I had already paid the amount owing. I told her that I was still waiting in line to make payment. She then advised me that they had given me a R10,000 graduation rebate. This was something that PHD graduates qualified for. This meant that I only had to pay R16,000. I was so grateful for that and made sure I paid and then took the proof of payment directly to the finance office without wasting any time. It was the greatest news ever: my account had been cleared and I could finally graduate. I was the happiest person on Earth because I finally got to achieve what I had worked so hard for over the years. Remember, due to delays caused by third parties, I had to graduate in 2017 whereas I registered in 2007, which is 10 years, even though I finished everything in 2014. Mind you, three years were wasted due to problems with the account at the university. I kept my cool and went with it because I knew what was waiting ahead. Talk about patience hey. I would've probably given up if I was someone else. In fact, I know a number of people who have given up on their dreams to achieve their Master's degree due to third part jealousy. I told myself that I would never let anyone stand in my way of achieving what I set myself out to achieve, not now, not ever. That is why I pushed so hard to get the university to complete the process and allow me to graduate.

In April 2017, the final day was announced and we were busy with preparations to ensure that when the day came, I would be ready for it. I have never given up, not once and I thanked myself for the patience I had to see myself up to where I am. When I look back at the difficulties I had to endure, I smile because it meant that I have resilience to withstand the hardships that I have been through. I was singing *I am a survivor* in my heart, lol. I wish to share this journey with as many people as possible who are on the verge of giving up on their dreams. I want to say to them: this is doable. You can achieve anything if you put your mind to it. As I complete my journey towards starting my career on a different note, I am aspiring to become a professor in the future as I want to remain within the academic space after I retire from my current occupation. However, I am already assisting a few individuals with their studies and it brings me so much joy to see them achieve their goals and their dreams becoming a reality. I normally like to challenge individuals to study as this creates a platform to discuss and debate on issues that will help bring about change in our communities. I would like to see more researchers in the EMS line of work in the future as we have very few of those in the country so that we can make very meaningful contributions to the industry. Whatever information we can gather through research, will go a long way to contribute to the change in our service for the better.

I would also like to challenge anyone out there in the industry who believes they can make a meaningful contribution to the lives of EMS workers in the country. Please come forward with whatever information that you have and together let us build a better EMS for the people of our country. Together, we can build a better future for our children who want to venture into the EMS field.

The Closing Chapter

I just want to say to all the readers, that I wrote this book for two reasons. The first reason is that I want to encourage those who think that when you have your heart set on a career path and it doesn't work, it means that it is the end. Look at my journey. I wanted to become an architect and interior designer, which is something I loved so passionately. However, because of powers beyond my control, I ended up in the military and studying in the medical field, which is something I never ever dreamt I could go into. I then decided to make the most of the situation and strove to become better at what I was doing. I then became a very confident lecturer in my field which saw me having the confidence to stand in front of a class without preparation but still manage to deliver a flawless lecture. I call that an achievement and I believe it can be done with the right attitude. The right attitude changes everything.

The second reason why I wrote the book is because I wanted to share with the readers that no matter how difficult and challenging it can be, no matter how many obstacles you might come across in your journey, never ever give up, especially when you want to make it a success. I have gone through a lot and there were times when I felt like throwing in the towel and call it quits. However, there was a little voice inside me that kept on saying to me, "Remember why you are doing this. You want to make a difference and also want to be the first in your family to graduate." So, this kept me pushing against all odds. I have had people saying to me that they do not think they could have the heart and patience that I have to hold on for so long. Even when I told people that I want to write a book and share my struggles, many of them kept on saying to me, "You really have the heart and the patience. We would have given up long ago." The answer that I gave all of them is, "If you really want something and you want it that bad, you fight for it until you have it and here I am, a qualified Doctoral degree graduate and the first in the entire family (which extends to both my mother and my father's side)." I am proud to be representing both surnames – Sibanda and Petersen – because these are the two surnames that brought me into this earth to make a difference in the lives of others. This is a beginning of another journey for me, a journey of helping those who think that it is impossible, those who are on the verge of giving up. I am here to give you the courage and possibly share something to take home, which might make you see your career choice from a different light going forward.

With these few words I would like to thank all those who have encouraged and supported me during my journey and those who had faith in me, when I didn't have faith in myself (trust me I had those moments). They kept telling me that I am going to make it and I should never give up. This book is the result of finally making it as I had always wanted to write one and publish it for people to read about my journey. ***From Soldier to Doctor: A Journey Through Life of Hardship and Hard Work*** is for all of you and I hope that you have enjoyed the read.

Lastly, I want to also thank my late wife (God rest her soul) for having my back at all times. You were my pillar of strength and you kept up with the late nights and less time spent together and sometimes my absence but never even gave up. I am so grateful for all the support and encouragement and being the mother and father in my periods of absence.

~The End~

www.ingramcontent.com/pod-product-compliance
Lightning Source LLC
Chambersburg PA
CBHW071459130726
47997CB00006B/2404